The Living Self

Feeling Fully Alive in an

Over-Institutionalized World

(in 550 words or less)

by
Alec Tramposch

ISBN 978-0-9968213-7-7
kaerlud-301@yahoo.com
www.TheLivingSelf.org

The
Living
Self

I.

1.

The first step to feeling fully alive in an
over-institutionalized world,

is to understand why we do or
do not feel fully alive.

2.

Each of us is made up of

a living self,

an institutional identity.

3.

In our living self:

We are born.

We eat, drink, sleep, breathe,
poop, pee, procreate.

We have parents, siblings, children,
friends, acquaintances.

We get sick, we recover.

We feel joy and we laugh.
We feel sad and we cry.

We sing, we dance, we enjoy nature.
We talk, we think, we work, we pray.

We have talent.
We have a personality.

We live. We love. We die.

The living self is who we are as living beings.

4.

Our institutional identity is the totality
of information about us:

> name, birthdate, driver's license,
>
> passport, education, marital status,
>
> cell phone, email, social media page,
>
> work history, position title,
>
> income, bank account, property ownership,
>
> religious affiliation, association
> memberships, political party,
>
> last will, obituary, eulogy, biography.

The institutional identity is made from words. It is
created. It is learned. It enables us to be an active
part of a culture of civilized institutions.

II.

5.

Only the living self is alive.

As living beings, we are alive.

6.

Institutions and institutional identity are useful and necessary, but they are not alive.

Institutions are agreed-upon rules of behavior for the people who make up the institution or are affected by it.

Institutions are made up of living beings, but institutions themselves are not alive.

7.

Our well-being resides only in our living self.

> Since only living beings are alive, while institutions and institutional identities are not, our well-being can only be found in our living self, and in our ties to other living beings and the natural world.

8.

The proper role of institutions and institutional identity is to nurture the well-being of living beings and their personal communities.

> We originally created institutions to help attain our well-being, better than nature could do on her own.

In short, institutions are tools to serve the well-being of the living self.

9.

Over-institutionalization occurs when institutions fail to perform that role, and instead become the beneficiaries of civilized culture at the expense of living beings.

10.

If in response to over-institutionalization, we start to identify with our institutional identity and seek our well-being there, we may cease to feel fully alive.

> When the benefits of civilization go to institutions and the institutional identity, they become more important than our living self.

> Our well-being is not fulfilled.

> We are separated from our true self and from each other.

III.

11.

We tend to feel fully alive when:

> We maintain a balance of living self
> and institutional identity.

> We look for our well-being in our living self.

12.

We tend not to feel fully alive when:

> We neglect the living self.

> We look for our well-being in institutions
> and institutional identity.

13.

We my be able to go from not feeling fully alive
to feeling fully alive in any situation by asking:

Is my living self involved?

Is the well-being of my living self, and
that of others, being served?

Are my interactions with others
living self to living self, or
institutional identity to institutional identity?

The Living Self

If our living self is present and involved;

If it participates and benefits in every situation; then

We feel fully alive

(even in an over-institutionalized world)

Contact and Comments:

kaerlud-301@yahoo.com

www.TheLivingSelf.org

Made in the USA
Las Vegas, NV
07 February 2021